Birthday Book Club

This book was donated
in honor of the birthday of

Katie Thayer

by

Her family

February 2, 2004

The Science of Living Things

What is a
Horse?

Bobbie Kalman & Heather Levigne

 Crabtree Publishing Company

www.crabtreebooks.com

The Science of Living Things Series
A Bobbie Kalman Book

(Dedicated by Heather Levigne)
For April - a sister and friend

Editor-in-Chief
Bobbie Kalman

Writing team
Bobbie Kalman
Heather Levigne

Editors
John Crossingham
Niki Walker

Copy editors
Amanda Bishop
Kathryn Smithyman
Heather Fitzpatrick

Computer design
Kymberley McKee Murphy

Production coordinator
Heather Fitzpatrick

Photo researcher
Heather Levigne

Photographs
Bob Langrish: front cover, pages 1, 4, 5, 6, 8, 10, 11 (top),
    13, 14, 15, 16, 17, 18-19, 20-21, 22, 23, 29, 30, 31
Other images by Adobe Image Library and Digital Stock

Illustrations
Barbara Bedell: page 28
Jeanette McNaughton-Julich: pages 4, 6, 9 (top and middle),
    10 (top), 14, 20
Margaret Amy Reiach: pages 7, 22, 25, 27
Bonna Rouse: pages 8, 9 (bottom), 10 (middle and bottom)

Separations and film
Embassy Graphics

Printer
Worzalla Publishing

Crabtree Publishing Company

www.crabtreebooks.com   1-800-387-7650

PMB16A
350 Fifth Avenue
Suite 3308
New York, NY
10118

612 Welland Avenue
St. Catharines
Ontario
Canada
L2M 5V6

73 Lime Walk
Headington
Oxford
OX3 7AD
United Kingdom

Cataloging in Publication Data
Kalman, Bobbie
    What is a horse?
        p. cm. -- (The Science of living things)
        Includes index.
        ISBN 0-86505-984-5 (library bound) ISBN 0-86505-961-6 (pbk.)
    This book introduces children to the physiology of horses, zebras, and other equines, including their behavior in the wild.
        1. Horses—Juvenile literature. [1. Horses.] I. Levigne, Heather. II. Title. III. Series: Kalman, Bobbie. Science of living things.
SF302.K35 2001
636.1—dc21

LC00-069358
CIP

Contents

What is a horse?

Horses belong to a group of animals called **mammals**. Mammals are **warm-blooded animals**, which means their body temperature stays the same in both hot and cold surroundings.

The first horses

Millions of years ago, horses were much smaller. They roamed freely in large **herds**. People hunted them for their meat and used their hides to make clothing.

Domesticating the horse

Scientists are not certain when humans began **domesticating**, or taming, horses. Some scientists think that about 14 000 years ago, people began using horses to carry heavy loads. They soon realized that horses could also carry people. Traveling on horseback allowed people to cover greater distances in less time. Hunting on horseback was also much easier than hunting on foot.

Modern horses

Today, people use horses in many ways. Some horses work with people on farms. Others are raised for riding or racing. In some parts of the world, horses roam freely in the wild. Most "wild" horses are not truly wild, however. They are domesticated horses that have escaped or have been released into the wilderness. These animals are called **feral** horses.

Przewalski's horse is the only type of horse that is classified as a true wild horse. Even though these horses have lived in zoos, they have never been tamed.

The horse family tree

Horses, ponies, asses, and zebras belong to the **equine** family. People **breed** horses in order to create animals that are suited for racing, pulling heavy loads, or doing other kinds of work.

Small, medium, or large?

Horses can be divided into groups based on their appearance and size. Ponies are the smallest horses. Light horses, such as Thoroughbreds and Arabians, are used for riding and racing. **Draft** horses are the largest. They are often used for very heavy work, such as pulling farm equipment. Clydesdales and Shires are two popular types of draft horses.

The horse ancestor

Some scientists think that horses are descended from a mammal that was about the size of a medium-sized dog. This animal, called *Hyracotherium*, had a short neck, slender legs, and large, pawlike feet. Its front feet had four toes, and its hind feet had three. Over millions of years, the body of this mammal slowly changed. It grew larger, and its legs became longer. Most of its toes became smaller until only a single large toe remained, which formed a hoof. This one-toed horse was called *Equus*.

(left) Large draft horses are very strong. They are able to pull farm equipment and carry heavy loads. This horse is plowing a field with a farmer.

The equine family

The equine family is made up of the horse, two species of asses, and three species of zebras. All these animals are descended from *Equus*.

Arabian

Clydesdale

pony

Horses

Although there is only one horse species, there are over 200 different **breeds**.

Asses

There are two species of asses: the African ass and the Asiatic ass.

African ass

Asiatic ass

Zebras

There are three species of zebras: the plains zebra, the mountain zebra, and Grevy's zebra.

plains zebra

mountain zebra

Grevy's zebra

A horse's body

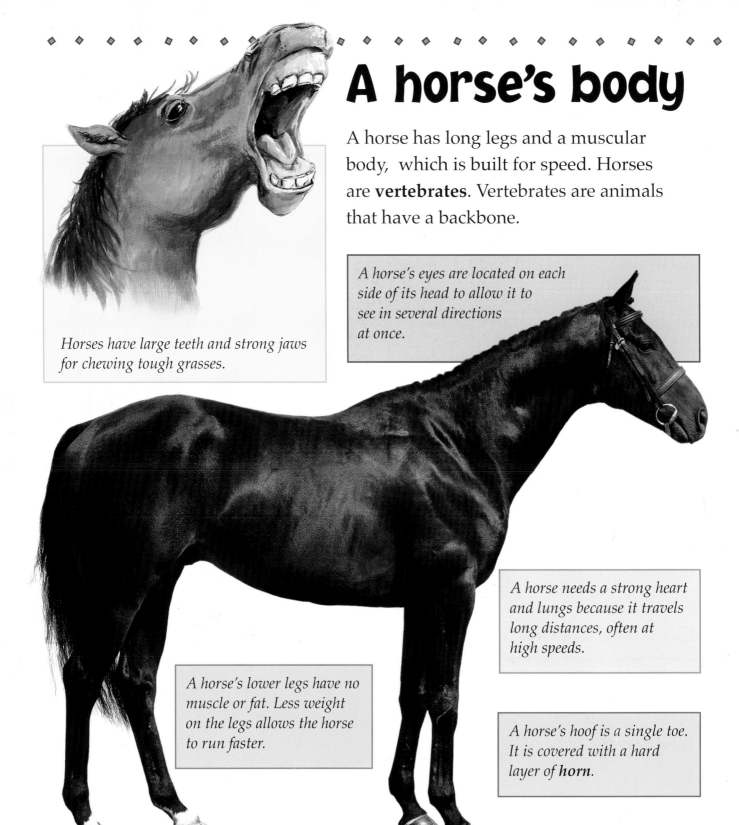

A horse has long legs and a muscular body, which is built for speed. Horses are **vertebrates**. Vertebrates are animals that have a backbone.

Horses have large teeth and strong jaws for chewing tough grasses.

A horse's eyes are located on each side of its head to allow it to see in several directions at once.

A horse needs a strong heart and lungs because it travels long distances, often at high speeds.

A horse's lower legs have no muscle or fat. Less weight on the legs allows the horse to run faster.

*A horse's hoof is a single toe. It is covered with a hard layer of **horn**.*

Colors and markings

Horses come in many colors, including black, **bay**, gray, and chestnut. Some colors have interesting names, such as **skewbald**, **strawberry roan**, and **fleabitten gray**. Many horses also have white markings on their coat. In the wild, these patterns and colors help horses blend in with their surroundings and hide from enemies. Domesticated horses are often bred for certain colors or markings.

*This horse has a light bay coat and a small mark called a **snip** on its nose.*

*The coat of this horse is dark bay, or brown. The diamond-shaped mark on its forehead is called a **star**.*

*This horse has a black coat with a **blaze**, which is a wide stripe from the forehead to the tip of the nose.*

*This horse has a chestnut coat with a **stripe** down the center of its nose.*

Give 'em a hand

Horses are measured in **hands**. One hand is equal to four inches (10 cm). The term "hand" comes from the way people measured horses many years ago, using their hand as a ruler.

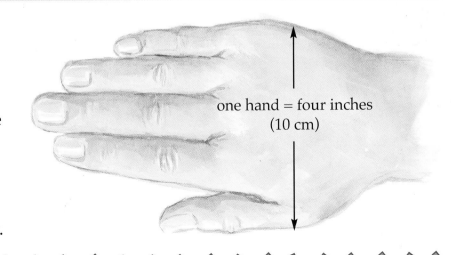

one hand = four inches (10 cm)

Horse sense

Horses are highly sensitive animals. A horse's senses of smell, sight, taste, touch, and hearing are well developed. Horses use their senses to gather information about their surroundings. Their senses also help them communicate with their mates, young, and other members of their herd. Good senses help horses stay alert and avoid danger, even when their head is lowered while they **graze**. Some people are said to have "horse sense." What do you think this expression means?

Now ear this!

A horse's ears are always moving. Pointing the ears in different directions helps a horse focus on a specific sound. The position of a horse's ears also provides clues about its mood. People who work with horses pay attention to these clues in order to avoid frightening or angering their horse. Wild horses use their ears to send one another messages.

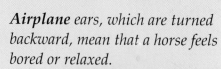

Airplane ears, which are turned backward, mean that a horse feels bored or relaxed.

*When a horse is alert and interested, its ears are **pricked** forward to catch sounds.*

Ears that droop out to the sides and face downward can mean that the horse is tired or sick.

***Pinned** ears show that a horse is angry or aggressive. Watch out!*

Sight

A horse's eyes are placed on either side of its head. This position allows the horse to see almost all the way around. It is very difficult to sneak up on a horse without being seen!

Smell

Horses have a very good sense of smell. They use scent to send and receive messages within their herd. For example, **mares** that are **in season** give off a scent to tell male horses that they are ready to mate. Mares also use scent to mark their young and identify them among a group of other **foals**.

(top) A horse's nose, lips, and ears are very sensitive to touch. When two horses meet, they often rub and lick each other's muzzle to send friendly messages.

When a horse is startled, it uses all of its senses to gather information about the situation. It pricks its ears forward, opens its eyes wide, and flares its nostrils.

Foals

A mare is pregnant for 11-13 months before she gives birth to a **foal**. While giving birth, the mother and her newborn are easy targets for **predators**. Most mares wait until nighttime to deliver their baby. They leave the rest of the herd to find a dark quiet place where they will not be disturbed and where they will be safe from enemies.

A foal is born

To have her baby, the mare lies down on her side. The foal leaves its mother's body front feet first. It is born with its eyes open. The mare stands up and starts licking her baby's face and body to clean the foal. After the foal is clean, the mare and foal rest together for a short time.

Bonding with baby

Cleaning the baby's body after birth allows the mother horse to bond with her baby. She learns how to identify her foal by its scent, even when the baby is among other foals. The foal also learns its mother's scent.

Drink your milk

Like all mammals, female horses make milk in their body to feed their baby. This milk contains important nutrients that help the baby grow strong and healthy. Foals begin drinking milk from their mother's body right after they are born.

A mare feeds and protects her foal until it is about a year old. This newborn foal is a bit shaky on its feet.

Growing strong

Foals develop very quickly. They can gallop, play, scratch and groom themselves, and even swim only one day after they are born! As they grow older, they sleep less and spend more time grazing and playing with other foals. During this time, they learn how to become a part of their herd.

Where do horses live?

Horses live all over the world. Some have **migrated** to different areas on their own, but most have been transported by humans. As people moved from place to place, they took their domesticated animals with them. Horses have **adapted**, or become suited, to many different habitats. They can live in almost any environment because people take care of them.

Icelandic horses are well-adapted to their environment. Their sturdy body keeps them sure-footed as they wander across the steep, frozen landscape of Iceland.

Camargue horses

Camargue horses live in large herds in the south of France. They are known as the "horses of the sea" because they live near the ocean. Their diet is made up of coarse grasses, reeds, and salt water.

People allow camargue horses to roam freely most of the time. They are known as **semi-wild** horses, which means they are not kept in fenced areas. Once a year, however, the Camargue horses are rounded up by local farmers and inspected to make sure they are healthy.

At birth, Camargue horses are dark gray or brown. As they get older, their coat turns bright white.

The wild ones

When Spanish settlers came to the western United States, they brought horses with them. Some of these horses escaped and reproduced in the wild. They became known as **mustangs**. The name "mustang" comes from *musteno*, which is a Spanish word that means "wild." Cowboys often tried to tame these "wild" horses to use them for herding cattle.

Cowboys in the Old West needed horses to travel between towns and to help manage large cattle herds.

Life in a herd

A horse's strongest **instinct** is to be part of a herd, or group, of other horses. Herds offer protection from predators. Horses also need companionship. They are happiest when they are around other horses!

Horse society

A wild herd may contain between three and thirty horses. Each herd has one **stallion**, several mares, and their foals. It is the stallion's job to keep the herd together and prevent other stallions from joining. The mares protect their young and keep the herd moving in search of food.

Home on the range

Horses spend much of their time wandering around their home range. This area usually covers about 30 to 80 square miles (78 to 207 km²). The herd often walks in single file and stops occasionally to eat, drink, and sleep. Most herds follow the same familiar paths over and over again.

To show affection for the members of their herd, horses often groom one another. They use their teeth to rub and scratch each other on the back.

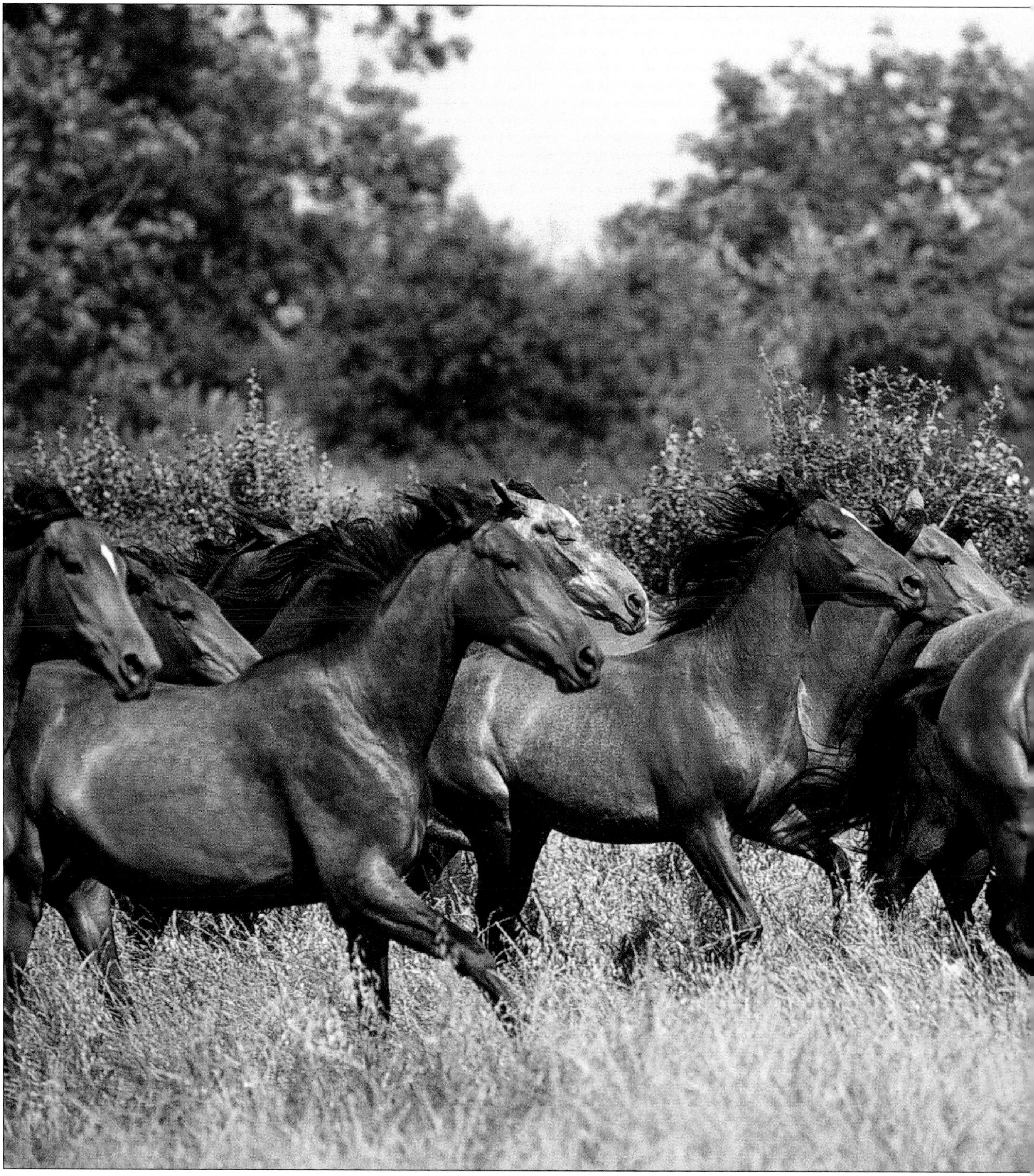

On the move

Horses have four different **gaits**, or paces at which they move. The **walk** is the slowest gait. **Trotting** is slightly quicker than walking. The **canter** is a slow run, and the **gallop** is a fast run. Galloping is the fastest gait, but wild horses rarely run at a full gallop unless there is a predator chasing them.

The fastest horse

The fastest breed of horse is the quarter horse. Its name comes from its ability to gallop at top speed for a quarter of a mile (1.6 km). Quarter horses often run as fast as 25 miles (40 km) per hour. They also have good reflexes and are able to stop and turn quickly. Thoroughbreds can run longer distances, but they do not usually run faster than 19 miles (30 km) per hour. Still, they are the best horses for racing.

Horses stick together as a herd, even when they are running!

Horse food

Horses spend most of their time grazing on plants such as grass and hay. These foods are difficult to break down and contain few nutrients. Grazing animals have large, flat teeth, which they use to chew their food slowly. They need to eat large amounts of food in order to get as many nutrients as possible.

Digesting food

Cows and giraffes chew a **cud**, which helps them **digest** their food. They chew and swallow a mouthful of grass, and then they bring it back up from their stomach to rechew it. When they swallow it a second time, their body  absorbs the nutrients more easily. Horses, however, do not chew a cud. They have a small stomach, so they eat tiny meals several times a day. By eating this way, they are able to digest their food more easily.

Horses like to eat a varied diet, including fruits, berries, flowers, nuts, and many different plants. When they feed near water, they pull up plants from the riverbed.

Ponies

A pony is any horse that is under 14.2 hands high. Ponies live all over the world. Britain is home to more **indigenous**, or native, ponies than any other country. It has nine indigenous breeds. They are known as Mountain and Moorland ponies because they are originally from rough mountainous regions in England, Scotland, and Ireland. Shetland ponies, shown above, are originally from Scotland. At less than seven hands, they are the smallest pony breed.

Exmoor ponies

Some scientists think that the Exmoor pony has lived in England for millions of years. This pony has not been **crossbred**, or mated with other pony breeds, so it has changed very little since prehistoric times. In order to live in their harsh habitat, Exmoor ponies have several special adaptations.

They have a thick, double-textured coat to keep out the cold. They also have special eyelids that form a protective hood over their eyes to keep out wind and snow. Exmoor ponies have a larger head than that of other ponies. When they breathe in cold air, the air takes longer to travel to their lungs, allowing it more time to become warm.

*To feed themselves in winter, Exmoor ponies must dig up plant bulbs and roots. In summer, they feed mainly on wild grasses and **bracken**. Bracken is a fern that is poisonous to other animals such as sheep.*

Asses and donkeys

Asses are small, long-eared cousins of horses. Donkeys are asses that have been tamed. They are divided into four groups according to their size: Miniature donkeys, which stand up to nine hands; Standard donkeys, which stand between nine and twelve hands; Large Standards, which stand between twelve and fourteen hands; and Mammoth or Jack Stock donkeys, which stand over fourteen hands.

Different from horses

Donkeys are smaller than most horses. They weigh between 400 and 600 pounds (180 and 270 kg) and can grow up to 44 inches (1.12 m) tall. Donkey ears are longer than horse ears, whereas donkey manes and tails are shorter. Most donkeys have gray hair, but some have black or white coats. A line called a **shoulder-cross** runs down their back and across their shoulders.

Rugged animals

Unlike horses, donkeys do not suffer from many diseases. Donkeys also require much less grooming than horses do, to stay clean and healthy. They need only to have their toenails clipped three times a year!

What did you call me?

Donkeys have many names. A female donkey is called a **jennet** or **jenny**, and a male donkey is known as a **jack**. Sometimes donkeys are crossbred with horses. If a male donkey mates with a female horse, the offspring is called a **mule**. The offspring of a male horse and a female donkey is called a **hinny**. These new breeds are often larger, stronger, and sturdier than their parents, but they are **sterile**, which means they cannot produce offspring of their own.

Spanish explorers brought burros to Mexico. Burro is the Spanish name for a donkey. Some burros escaped and crossed the border into the southwestern United States, becoming the first American donkeys.

Zebras

All three species of zebras live in Africa. Some inhabit the grasslands, whereas others live in dry mountain areas. Zebras are smaller than horses. Like asses, they have a short, upright mane, long ears, and a tufted tail.

Searching for food

Zebras feed on tall, coarse grasses. Some zebras also eat shrubs, herbs, and plant bulbs. During the rainy season on the plains, many zebras must migrate to find food.

Why do zebras have stripes?

In the past, some scientists thought that the zebra's stripes provided camouflage from predators. In fact, zebras are found mainly in open grassland areas where there is little vegetation with which they could blend in. Today, scientists are still not sure why zebras are striped. Some think that the striped pattern may prevent insects from bothering the animals. Others think that the stripes are as unique as finger-prints, and each zebra can be identified by its striped pattern. Scientists are still trying to figure out why zebras are striped. Give your opinion about why zebras might need their stripes!

Few enemies

Most horses have few natural enemies because they live near people. In the wild, however, predators such as lions and wolves prey on feral horses. Horses defend themselves from enemies by staying together in herds and keeping a close watch on their surroundings at all times.

Wolves are cunning hunters. A wolf pack can catch a sick or young horse easily.

Safety in numbers

Predators are more likely to attack a single horse than charge into a herd. Foals stay near the middle of the herd, as shown below, so they are protected on all sides. Old or weak horses that cannot keep up with the herd fall behind and become easy targets for predators. Horses that run too far ahead of the herd are also at risk of being attacked.

Fight or flight?

In a dangerous situation, a horse's best defense is its speed. Most horses run from an enemy as fast as possible. Sometimes, however, a horse must stand its ground and fight. It thrusts its head out, bares its teeth, and lunges forward in order to appear threatening. If a predator gets too close, a horse will strike out with a sharp, heavy hoof.

These female horses surround their foals to protect them from natural enemies. If a predator gets too close, the mares will defend the foals by kicking the enemy.

Horsin' around

Have you ever wondered how horses sleep? Do you know why horses roll around on the ground? Read on to find out why horses love to "horse around!"

Why do horses roll on the ground?

Horses roll for many reasons. If their back is itchy, rolling helps scratch it. Rolling also helps shed loose hair. Often, horses in a herd roll in the same spot. Their scents combine on that spot to form one unique odor. By rolling in this scent, the horses identify themselves as part of the herd. Sometimes horses roll on the ground if they have stomach pain.

Movies often show horses rearing up on their hind legs. Male horses sometimes rear up when they are fighting, but this behavior is rare.

How do horses sleep?

Horses do not spend much time sleeping—they are always on the lookout for predators that might try to sneak up on them. Sometimes horses sleep standing up so they will be ready to run if an enemy approaches. In order to sleep deeply, however, a horse must lie down on its side.

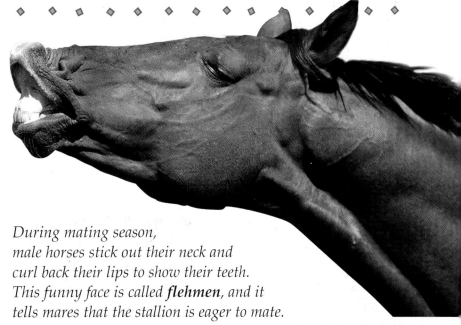

*During mating season, male horses stick out their neck and curl back their lips to show their teeth. This funny face is called **flehmen**, and it tells mares that the stallion is eager to mate.*

Sometimes horses need to stretch out and sleep on their side or stomach. If they do not sleep, they become tired and cranky—just as people do when they do not get enough rest!

Words to know

adapt To become different to suit a new environment

breed (n) The name for a particular type of horse; (v) To have two similar horses mate in order to produce offspring with the same characteristics, such as speed, size, color or strength

crossbreed To have horses of different breeds or species mate with one another

digest To break down food so that the body can use it for energy

domesticate To tame a wild animal

equine Relating to a family of animals that includes horses, ponies, asses, and zebras

feral Describing an animal that was once tame but now lives and hunts in the wild

flehmen A facial expression used by male horses to attract females during mating

gait One of the many ways in which a horse moves its legs as it walks or runs

instinct Knowledge of how to do something without being taught

mare in season A female horse that is ready to mate

mate To make babies

migrate To move from one location to another in order to mate or find food or water

predator An animal that kills and eats other animals

sterile Describing an animal that cannot make babies

vertebrate An animal that has a backbone

warm-blooded Describing an animal whose body temperature does not change with the temperature of its surroundings

Index

1 2 3 4 5 6 7 8 9 0   Printed in the U.S.A.   0 9 8 7 6 5 4 3 2 1